Growing up Safe

Safety

at school

Illustrated by Sue Wilkinson

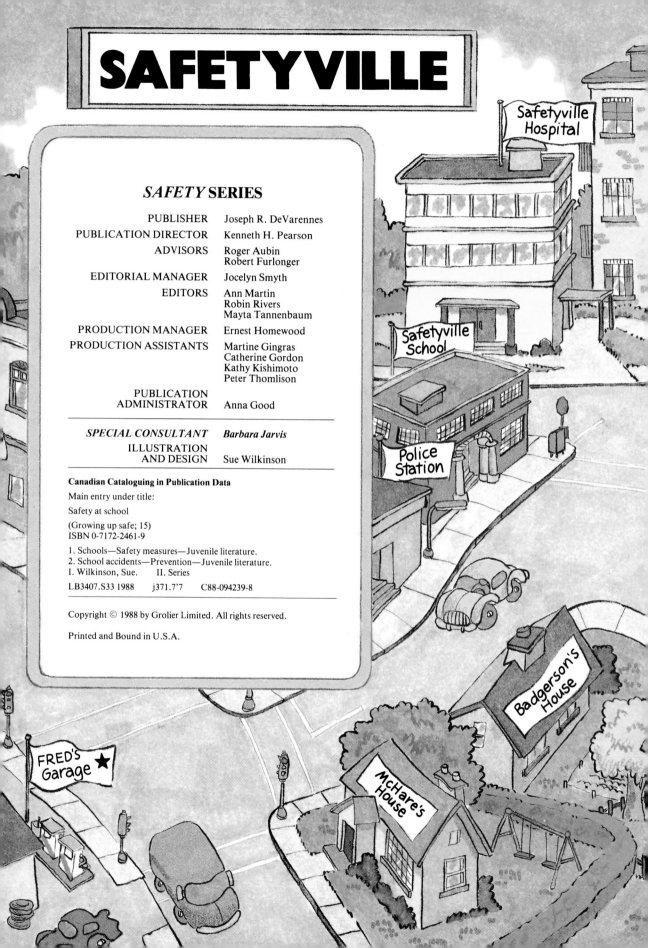

SAFETYVILLE

SAFETY SERIES

PUBLISHER	Joseph R. DeVarennes
PUBLICATION DIRECTOR	Kenneth H. Pearson
ADVISORS	Roger Aubin
	Robert Furlonger
EDITORIAL MANAGER	Jocelyn Smyth
EDITORS	Ann Martin
	Robin Rivers
	Mayta Tannenbaum
PRODUCTION MANAGER	Ernest Homewood
PRODUCTION ASSISTANTS	Martine Gingras
	Catherine Gordon
	Kathy Kishimoto
	Peter Thomlison
PUBLICATION ADMINISTRATOR	Anna Good

SPECIAL CONSULTANT	Barbara Jarvis
ILLUSTRATION AND DESIGN	Sue Wilkinson

Canadian Cataloguing in Publication Data

Main entry under title:

Safety at school

(Growing up safe; 15)
ISBN 0-7172-2461-9

1. Schools—Safety measures—Juvenile literature.
2. School accidents—Prevention—Juvenile literature.
I. Wilkinson, Sue.   II. Series

LB3407.S33 1988   j371.7'7   C88-094239-8

Skunkerton's House

RIVER PARK

Raccoonelli's House

Bearberry's House

Sweet's Bakery

Safetyville Fire Hall

Rita's Dress Shop

Skunkerton Family

Mom   Alex Sarah

Come join Alex and Sarah Skunkerton as they find out everything they need to know about safety at school.

OBEY THE CROSSING GUARD.

The school bell is about to ring. Don't dawdle.

DO NOT RUN IN THE HALLS OR STAIRWAYS.

DO NOT PUT CRAYONS, MARKERS, CHALK OR PENCILS IN YOUR MOUTH. THEY MAY HARM YOU.

USE SCISSORS SAFELY. NEVER RUN WITH THEM IN YOUR HAND AND ALWAYS PASS THEM HANDLES FIRST.

TELL YOUR TEACHER IF YOU OR A CLASSMATE GET HURT.

THE SCHOOL NURSE HELPS YOU TO STAY SAFE.

DON'T STAND ON CHAIRS OR TABLES. ASK THE TEACHER FOR HELP.

ALWAYS LISTEN TO YOUR TEACHER. HE OR SHE CAN HELP YOU STAY SAFE.

IF THE FIRE ALARM RINGS DO WHAT THE TEACHER TELLS YOU TO.

TAKE TURNS ON PLAY EQUIPMENT.

DON'T PUSH OTHERS. YOU COULD HURT THEM.

DO NOT GO HOME WITH A STRANGER. TELL YOUR TEACHER IF SOMEONE YOU DON'T KNOW IS WAITING FOR YOU.

TELL YOUR PARENTS IF A TEACHER UPSETS YOU.